MISS PATCH'S Learn to Sew BOOK

MISS PATCH'S Learn to Sew BOOK

written by **Carolyn Meyer**   illustrated by **Mary Suzuki**

Houghton Mifflin Harcourt

Boston   New York

To Aunt Edith

CONTENTS

Chapter 6

Chapter 7

One

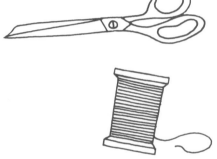

If your mother sews,
or your grandmother,
or your aunt,
or your older sister,
you are lucky.

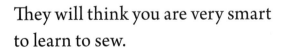

They will lend you their scissors,
and some needles and thread, and a thimble.
They might give you some pieces of cloth to work on.
And they can help you if you ever get stuck.

If no one at your house knows how to sew,
you are lucky.

They will think you are very smart
to learn to sew.

And they will never say,
"Here, let me show you how to do it."

This is Miss Patch. She is learning to sew.
You will see that if Miss Patch can sew, anyone can.
(Anyone except, of course, her dog Charlie.)
If you have two pieces of cloth,
you can sew them together to make something.

You can make a pillow.
You can make a big one for your father's chair,
or a fancy one for your bed,
or a little one for your doll's bed,
or even a very tiny one, with something inside smelling good,
for your mother's dresser drawer.

Miss Patch wants to make a pillow for Charlie.

HERE IS WHAT YOU NEED TO START

MATERIAL: It is easier to work on at first if it is smooth and not too heavy. It is more fun if it is pretty. Try to pick the kind that is nicest for the person you are sewing for.

GRANDMA

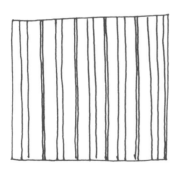

DADDY

CHARLIE

THREAD: When you are just beginning, use a bright color because it will not look so messy after you have worked with it. Use a color different from the cloth so that you can see what you have done. Next time you can use thread that is the same color as the cloth.

NEEDLES: A medium-sized one is good.

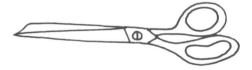

PINS: They hold things together while you sew. Keep them in a pincushion or stuck in a piece of paper. If your father sits on one, he might be angry.

SCISSORS: They should be sharp but not too big.

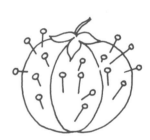

THIMBLE: Put it on the tallest finger of your sewing hand. Use it to push the needle through the cloth. It will feel funny, but you will get used to it, and then you will not want to sew without it.

BOX: Use any kind of box you have to keep your sewing things in. If you want, you can decorate it with crayons or fancy paper.

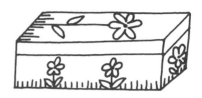

HANDS: Two of them. Clean ones are the best.

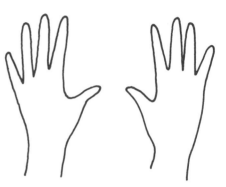

MEASURING TOOLS: A yardstick for measuring big things, like pieces of cloth, and a ruler for measuring small things, like seams, and a tape measure for going around things, like your waist. (If you don't have a tape measure, you can use a piece of plain cloth tape or string that doesn't stretch and measure it with a yardstick to see how much of the tape or string it takes to go around.)

THIS IS HOW TO MAKE THE PATTERN

If you have a pillow that is the right size, put it on a piece of newspaper. If the pillow has an old cover that comes off easily, put the cover on the paper instead. Draw around the pillow or pillow cover with a crayon. If you do not have a pillow, just draw the size you want to make.

If your drawing looks like this . . .
use a ruler or a piece of cardboard
to make straight edges.

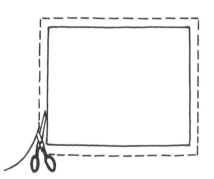

Then add about this much ——— (½″)
on each side for a seam and
draw another line.
You can use a different colored crayon.

Now cut out the pattern,
following the outside line.
Put the pattern on the floor
with the pillow in the center
and stand over it.
If you can see about
this much paper ——— (⅝″)
all around the pillow, it is just right.

THIS IS HOW TO CUT IT OUT

If you have one big piece of material, fold it in half.
If you have two smaller pieces of material, put one on top of
the other.

Then lay the pattern on top
and pin it.
Now cut all the way around the
pattern on the outside line.

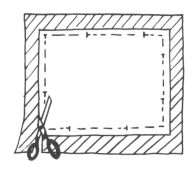

When you take out the pins, you will have one pattern and
two pieces of cloth.

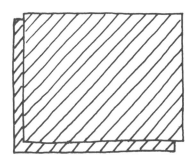

PATTERN

THIS IS HOW TO PUT IT TOGETHER

Put the pieces of cloth together like a sandwich. Be sure the right sides (the pretty sides) are on the inside where the butter would be. Now pin the "sandwich" together all the way around with the pinheads sticking out a little bit past the edge of the material.

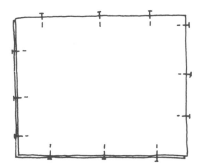

Remember that you added on this much ——— (½") to each side for a seam. Measure that much from the edge and make marks on the cloth to show you where to sew. You can use chalk on dark-colored cloth or pencil on light-colored cloth. It will look like this when you have finished marking.

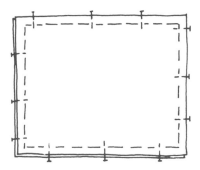

THIS IS HOW TO THREAD A NEEDLE

Cut a piece of thread as long as your arm.

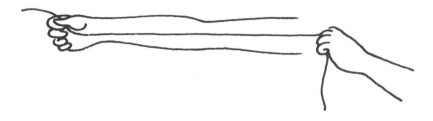

Then poke the end of the thread through
the "eye" of the needle.
It will go through more easily if you wet it on the tip of
your tongue and then squeeze it. Now try to hit the eye.
Pull the thread through until the ends are even
and make a knot.

This is how to make a knot:

Wet your finger a little on the
tip of your tongue.

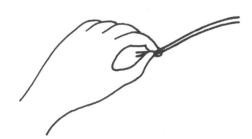

Wrap the thread around your
finger once.

Roll it off with your thumb.

Pull it tight.

The knot should be small and neat.
If it isn't, don't worry.
You can hide it so no one will see it,
and the next time you do it, it will look much better.

Miss Patch's knot looked like this:

But she tried again and again and at
last got one like this:

She thinks making a knot is the hardest part of sewing.
If you can do that, the rest will seem easy.

AND THIS IS HOW TO SEW

Hold your work like this if you are right-handed
(the other way around if you are left-handed).

Start in a corner and go ← that way.
Follow the chalk or pencil line you have drawn. Make one neat
stitch and pull the thread all the way through to the knot.
Pull it so that the thread lies flat.
But don't pull it so hard that you make a ruffle.

When you make several stitches
together, they are called running stitches.

Try to make your stitches small and all the same size.
See how it looks on the back.
It should look almost like this on both sides: — — — — — — — —

Miss Patch's stitches looked like this: ⸗ ⸗ ⸗ ⸗⸗‿⁓⸜⸝⸍⸌‿‿
But they got better   ⸗ ⸗⸍ ⸗‿⸗⸗⸗‿⸍‿⸗‿ ‿ ⸗
and better.   ⸗ ⸗ ⸗ ⸗⸗⸗ ⸗ ⸗ ⸗ ⸗

After you have sewed across one edge,
turn your work and keep going.
Then turn it again and do the next edge.

When you have sewed this far, fasten off the thread this way:
Take three extra little stitches right on top of each other
and cut the thread close to the material.
Turn the material right side out
and poke out the corners so that they are square.

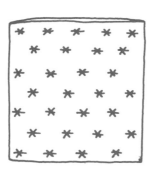

Now put the pillow inside.

You are not quite finished, but now you
can see how nice it will look.

If you do not have a pillow and are making your own stuffing,
it is time to find something to use for the stuffing.
Nylon stockings are good because you can wash the whole
pillow without taking out the stuffing.
Ask your mother to give you some that she is throwing away.

If you are making a tiny perfumed pillow for a drawer,
you will need some cotton sprinkled with a little perfume.
Be sure to *ask* if you may have some perfume.

When you have stuffed the pillow, turn to the inside the
two edges that are not sewed and pin them together.

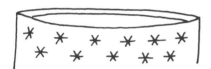
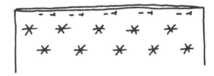

Do you have enough thread in your needle?
Make a knot in the end.

Put your needle in here
so that the knot is hidden.

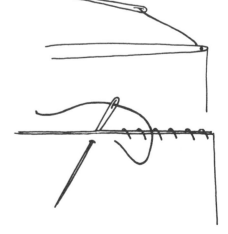

Then make little overcast
stitches like this.

When you come to the end, take three extra little stitches right on top of each other and cut the thread close to the material.

Now you have finished.

Charlie likes his new pillow.
How do you like yours?

There are lots of other things you can make
if you have two pieces of cloth.

You can make a drawstring bag to keep things in.
It can be as large or as small as you want to make it.

You can make a laundry bag for your sister
or a little bag for your brother's marbles and things.
You can make a beach bag for your friend
or a handbag to carry with your favorite dress.

Miss Patch is planning to make a shopping bag for herself
and a bone bag for Charlie.

After you have decided what kind of bag you are going to
make, you must find the right kind of material for it.

Sometimes you can find what you need right at home.

You can make a laundry bag from a sheet.
You can make a toy bag from a heavy shirt.
You can make a beach bag from a towel.
And if someone sewed your favorite dress for you,
there might be a piece left over for a matching bag.

But be careful!

If the sheet or the shirt or the towel is worn out,
your bag may be "worn out" too — before it is even finished.
And if the sheet or the shirt or the towel is still very good,
be sure to ask someone if it is all right for you to use it.

THIS IS HOW TO MAKE THE PATTERN

A newspaper is easy to use for a pattern.
You can fold it and cut it until you have the size you want.

A large sheet of newspaper is about the right size
for a laundry bag.
If you fold it in half, it is about the right size for a beach bag.
If you fold it again and cut it to make it square, it is about the
right size for a handbag or a bag for marbles.

Use a long ruler or yardstick and a crayon to draw the size you
want on the newspaper.

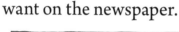

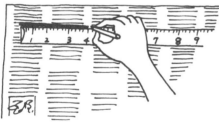

With another crayon add half
an inch on both sides and the
bottom for seams.
Add about an inch on top
for a casing — the place for
the drawstring to go through.
Now cut out the pattern on the outside lines.

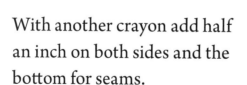

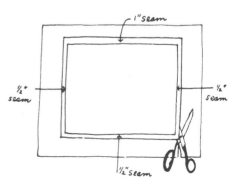

THIS IS HOW TO CUT IT OUT

If you have one big piece of material, fold it in half.
If you have two smaller pieces of material,
put one on top of the other.
Then lay the pattern on top and pin it.

Now cut all the way around the pattern on the outside lines,
just as you did for the pillow on page 8.

THIS IS HOW TO PUT IT TOGETHER

Take out the pins and put the two pieces of the bag
together again, like a sandwich.
Be sure the right sides are on the inside.
Pin it along the two sides and on the bottom.

Remember that you added half an inch on two sides and the
bottom for seams and 1 inch on top for a drawstring casing.

Measure from the edge and make marks
on the cloth to show you where to sew
the seams and the drawstring casing.
Measure half an inch from the mark you made
for a casing and make another set of marks
to show you where the drawstring will go.

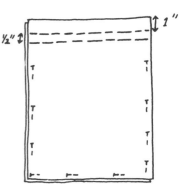

AND THIS IS HOW TO SEW

Thread your needle and knot the ends of the thread,
as you did for the pillow.
Start at the arrow and sew ← that way.

Sew only as far as the mark for the casing.
Fasten off the thread and cut it.

Then make another knot and begin again at the second mark.
Sew down the first side.
Turn your work and sew across the bottom.
Then turn your work and sew up the other side
as far as the first mark for the drawstring.
Fasten off the thread and cut it.

Make another knot
and begin again at the second mark for the drawstring.
This leaves an opening for pulling the drawstring
through the casing.

Sew right to the edge.
Fasten off the thread and cut it.

Now you are ready to make the
casing for the drawstring.

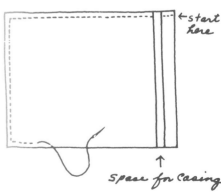

Keep the bag wrong side out.
Press open the seams on both sides,
with a warm iron or with your fingers.
Then fold down the hem on the top line
and press that.

Next turn under a little bit of the cut edge
and pin it all around.
It will be easier to handle if you baste it in place.
Basting is like the sewing you have been doing,
but the stitches are longer.
Use a different colored thread so you will know
which one to pull out when you are finished.

When you have basted all the way around
the hem, you can take out the pins.
Then thread your needle and make
one end of the thread longer than the other.
Put a knot in the long end of the thread.

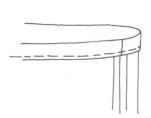

Now begin to make hemming stitches like this:

Fasten off the thread and cut it.
Pull out the basting thread.
Turn the bag right side out.
What are you going to use for a drawstring?

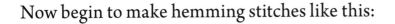

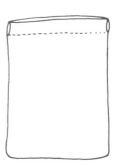

You can use ribbon for your handbag.
You can use rope for the laundry and beach bags.
You can use heavy cord or string for the marble bag.

You will need two pieces.

The pieces must be the same length — each one long enough
to go all the way around the bag with some left over.
And they must be narrow enough to go
through the space you have made.

You can fasten a safety pin to one end of
the drawstring and use that as a "needle"
to pull it through the drawstring space.
Put the drawstring through the opening
on one side and work it all the way around
and out through the same opening.
Then bring the ends together
and knot them.

Put the drawstring through the opening
on the opposite side and work it all the way around and out
through the same opening.
Then bring those ends together
and knot them.

Pull the strings and you're ready to go!

If you want to put a name on your bag,
you can do it this way:

Open the bag flat, right side out.
Then write the name in the center with pencil or chalk.
(This works best on plain material with no design.)
Now sew carefully around the letters with a backstitch:

Bring the needle up from the wrong side of the
material and take one small stitch — in and out.

Then put the needle in again exactly where it went in
for the first stitch and bring it out a little ahead of the
spot where the needle came out for the second stitch.
(It will seem that you are stitching backward —
and you are!)

Now put the needle in again exactly
where it went in for the second stitch.
You have made two backstitches.

Keep your hand under the top layer of material
so that you don't sew through both sides of the bag.
When you have stitched around the letters,
turn the bag inside out.

Fasten off the thread by winding the needle in and out
of the stitches on the wrong side.
Don't sew through the material to fasten off
or it will show on the right side.

Three

If you have some small pieces of cloth of different kinds,
you can make something in the shape of a triangle
that has two "right" sides: a kerchief for yourself,
or a scarf for your aunt, or an apron for your mother.

Miss Patch never throws away
anything she thinks she
might use someday.
Charlie believes it is better
to save bones.

THIS IS HOW TO MAKE THE PATTERN

A triangle is half of a square
cut like a peanut-butter sandwich.

First draw a square on a piece of newspaper.
For the kerchief draw a square that is
about 12 inches on each side.
For the scarf draw a square that is about 18 inches on each side.
For the apron draw a square that is about 22 inches on each side.

Draw a line from one corner of the square to
the opposite corner and cut the square in half.
Mark the corners 1, 2, and 3, like this:

See what kinds of material you can find.
Try to use a plain piece for one side
and a patterned piece for the other.
You can make each side of the kerchief
to match a different outfit.

You can make the scarf with warm material for winter
or with light material for spring or fall.
You can make one side of the apron plain and one side fancy,
but the material should be something that washes easily.

If you have some pieces of lace or rickrack or braid,
you can use them to decorate the triangles.

THIS IS HOW TO CUT IT OUT

Lay the pattern on the material.
Try to fit it so that the two short sides of the triangle
go in the same direction as the
lengthwise (up and down) threads
and crosswise (back and forth)
threads of the material.

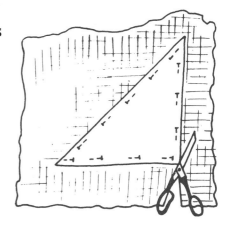

Pin the pattern and cut around it.

Use the same pattern to cut
another piece from a different
kind of material.

If you are making an apron and have enough cloth,
you can cut out two strips for the ties.
Make each strip about 4 inches wide
and about 16 inches long.
But if you do not have enough material for the ties,
you can use pieces of wide ribbon.

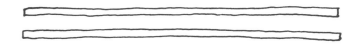

You can use narrow ribbon to tie the kerchief.

THIS IS HOW TO DECORATE IT

If you are going to decorate the kerchief or scarf or apron,
it is easier to do it before you sew the triangles together.

Here are some things you can do:
You can put rickrack around the edges of your kerchief.

Use pencil or chalk to draw light lines
on the right side of the material.
Draw the lines 2 inches in from the edge
along each side of the triangle. The lines
will cross each other in each corner.

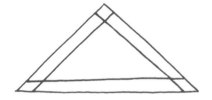

Lay the rickrack over the pencil lines
and follow the lines all the way
to the edge of the material.
Pin it and baste it.

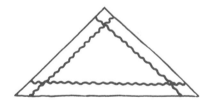

Sew the rickrack with running stitches
right down the middle.

You can decorate just one side
or put trimming on both sides of the kerchief.

You can put braid or lace around the edges of the neck scarf.
Pick a kind that goes well with the material you are using.
Follow the directions for putting rickrack on the kerchief,
but sew with small, neat hemming stitches
along both edges of the trimming.

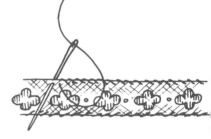

You can put a pocket on the apron.
Use material that matches either side
of the apron.
Cut it in the shape of a small triangle,
about 5 inches on each side.
Turn under about ¼ of an inch
on each edge.
Pin the edges and baste them.

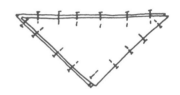

Then sew around the edges
with running stitches.

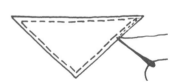

Lay the pocket on the apron.
Pin it in place and baste it.
Then sew it on two sides
with little hemming stitches.

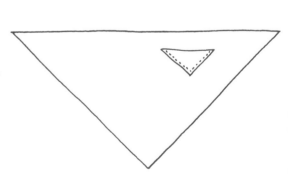

Don't forget to leave
the top open.

To make ties out of material for the apron,
turn a little bit of all the raw edges toward the wrong side of
each strip and press them with your fingers or a warm iron.
Baste around all the edges with a different colored thread.
Fold each strip in half the long way with the *wrong* side
on the inside and press the fold with your fingers.

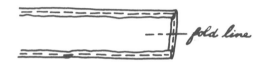

Pin the edges together so they are even.

Sew very close to the long edge and across the ends
with running stitches.

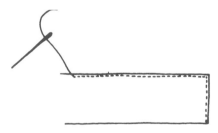

Fasten off the thread and cut it.

THIS IS HOW TO PUT IT TOGETHER

Put the two triangles together like a sandwich
with the right sides on the inside
and pin it all the way around.
Measure half an inch from each
edge for a seam.
Make marks on the cloth with
chalk or pencil to show you
where to sew.

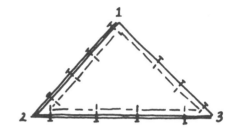

AND THIS HOW TO SEW

Thread your needle and knot the ends of the thread.
Start at corner 1 and sew to corner 2 with running stitches.
Make two extra stitches on top of each other
at the corner
to make it strong.
Then sew to corner 3.
Make two extra stitches.
When you are halfway from
corner 3 to corner 1, stop.

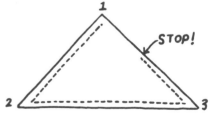

Fasten off the thread and cut it.

Trim off the points of the corners like this:
Turn the triangle right side out. Be careful
not to cut through your stitches.

Tuck in the edges that you did not sew
and press them and the rest of the edges
with your fingers or with a warm iron.
Pin and baste the opening.
Thread your needle and make one end of
the thread longer than the other.
Put a knot in the long end.
Sew the opening shut with little overcast stitches.
Try to make them so that you can hardly see them.
Fasten off the thread and cut it.
If your triangle is to be used as a
neck scarf, it is all finished.

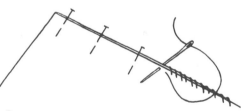

If you are going to wear the
triangle as a kerchief, you will
want to sew on narrow pieces of
ribbon to tie under your chin.
Choose ribbon about half an inch wide.
Cut two pieces about 10 inches long.
Cut one end of the ribbon straight
across and one end at an angle.

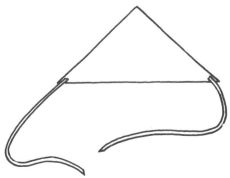

Turn under a little bit of the straight end.
Fasten it down with a few hemming stitches.
Sew that end to corner 2 of the triangle.
Make three or four stitches straight through
the ribbon and both layers of material.
Then sew the end of the ribbon in place
with tiny hemming stitches.
Sew the other piece of ribbon to corner 3.

If your triangle is to be an apron, you will want
to sew on the ties you have made or pieces of ribbon
about an inch wide and about 15 inches long.
Sew them on just as you did the ribbons for the kerchief.

Have you any other ideas for things to make with triangles?

Four

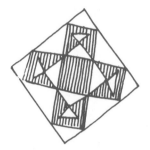

Long ago people saved scraps of material to
make warm covers for their beds.

Often they made beautiful designs with the
scraps and gave them pretty names like
Moon over the Mountain, Cats and Mice,
and Star of the Four Winds.

Sometimes they sewed odd-shaped pieces together
whichever way they would fit to make a Crazy Quilt.

Or they made a simple design of squares.

This is a good way to use leftovers
and to make something useful and pretty—
a patchwork cover for a pillow or even a little
patchwork quilt for a doll's bed or a baby's cradle
like the ones your great-grandmother might
have made when she was a girl.

IF YOU ARE GOING TO MAKE A PATCHWORK PILLOW

First decide how big the pillow will be.
You could make it 12 inches wide and 12 inches long.
You will need at least two different kinds of material.
You can use one plain and one with a design,
or you can use two designs if the colors are different.
If you have several different kinds of material,
that is all right, too.

THIS IS HOW TO MAKE THE PATTERN

Cut a square of cardboard 4 inches wide and 4 inches long.
Lay it on the material so that the sides of the square go in
the same direction as the threads of the material.
Draw around it with chalk or a sharp pencil.
If you are going to make only one side of the pillow cover
in patchwork, you will need to cut out 16 squares.
If you are going to make both sides in patchwork,
you will need to cut out 32 squares.
Try to cut an equal number of squares from
each kind of material.

THIS IS HOW TO PUT IT TOGETHER

Lay all of the patches out on a table, right side up (only half of them at a time if you are covering both sides of the pillow). Now arrange the patches so that the colors and patterns make a pretty design.

Lay them out like this:

Row 1   □   □   □   □

Row 2   □   □   □   □

Row 3   □   □   □   □

Row 4   □   □   □   □

Then collect them in rows, starting from the left.
Write the number of the row on a piece of paper
and pin it to the little pile of patches with a safety pin.

AND THIS IS HOW TO SEW

- -

Begin with row 1.
Put the first two patches together like a sandwich
with the right sides on the inside.
Pin one edge.
Measure a seam half an inch wide
and mark it with pencil or chalk.
Thread a needle, knot the ends together,
and sew the seam with small running stitches.

Open the "sandwich" and pin another patch
to one-half of the sandwich.
Measure a seam, mark it, and sew it.
Now there are three patches in a row.

Sew on another patch the same
way and make it four in a row.
Press the seams open with your
fingers or with a warm iron.
Pin the paper to the first patch
and put row 1 in a safe place.

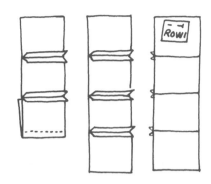

Then sew the next three rows in the same way.

Now take row 1 and row 2 and pin them together
with the right sides of the patches on the inside
to make a 1-o-n-g sandwich.
Measure a seam half an inch wide on the long edge
and mark it with pencil or chalk.
Sew it with small running stitches.
Then sew row 3 onto row 2 and sew row 4 onto row 3.
Press the seams open with your fingers or with a warm iron.

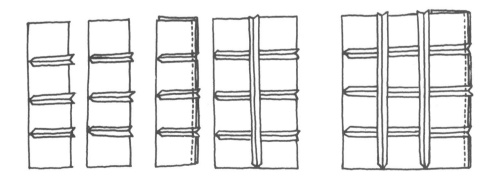

If you are making both sides of the pillow in patchwork, sew another block of squares in the same way. If you are making just one side of the pillow in patchwork, cut a piece of material the same size as the block of squares. Now turn back to page 12 and follow the directions for making a pillow.

Make the seams on each side half an inch wide.

IF YOU ARE GOING TO MAKE A COVER FOR YOUR DOLL'S BED

You could make one like this:

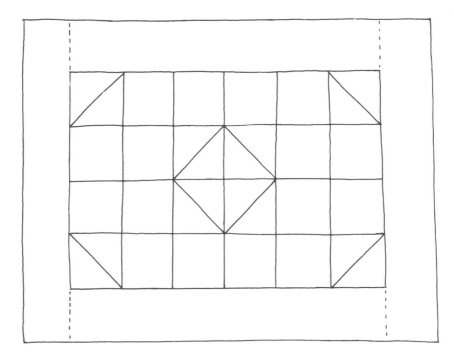

THIS IS HOW TO CUT IT OUT

You will need 24 patches.
Cut 16 patches 4 inches wide and 4 inches long.
Use as many different kinds of cloth
for the 4-inch patches as you want.
Cut 8 patches 4½ inches wide and 4½ inches long.
Use two different kinds of cloth and cut four of each kind.
Then cut each of these in half to make two triangles.

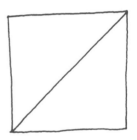

THIS IS HOW TO PUT IT TOGETHER

Put two *different* triangles together with
right sides on the inside and all the edges even.
Pin it, and measure a seam ⅜ of an inch
along the long edge.
Mark it with pencil or chalk.
Thread a needle, knot the ends together,
and sew the seam with small running stitches.
Make all the triangles back into squares in that way.

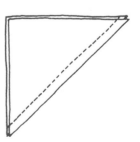

Now lay all the patches out on a table, right side up.
Put a triangle-square on each corner
and four triangle-squares in the center.
When you have all the patches arranged just the way you
want them, gather each row together, mark it with a number,
and fasten it with a safety pin.
You will have six rows with four patches in each row.

THIS IS HOW TO SEW

- -

Sew together the four patches in each row and then sew the
six rows together. Read page 36 again to see how to do it.
Make the seams half an inch wide. Next cut four pieces of
plain material, each one 4 inches wide and 19 inches long.
Sew one strip to each side. Then sew a strip
across the top and another one across the bottom.

If you want your doll to be very warm and you have an old
blanket that can be cut up (not wool, because it might shrink
in the wash), cut a piece 18 inches wide and 24 inches long
and pin it to the wrong side of the patches.
Then baste it all the way around.

Now cut a piece of material for the back,
19 inches wide and 25 inches long.
Put the cover together the way you did the pillow,
with the right sides on the inside,
and sew around three edges with running stitches.
Then turn it right side out and tuck in the raw edges —
the ones that have not been sewed.
Pin them and baste them.
Then sew with overcast stitches.

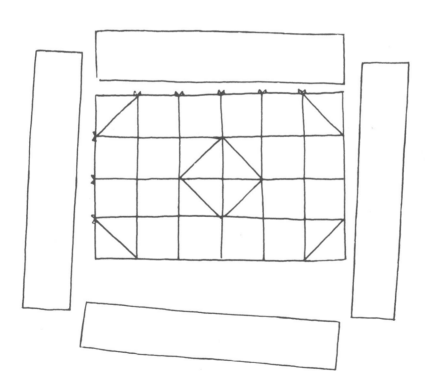

AND THIS IS HOW TO "QUILT" IT

Many years ago people decorated their patchwork covers
and made them stronger by sewing back and forth
over the whole thing with tiny
running stitches, sometimes
in a very fancy pattern.
This was called quilting.
But when they were in a hurry,
they had a faster way of holding
the layers together.
They made knots with yarn
every here and there.

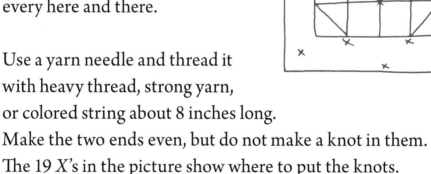

Use a yarn needle and thread it
with heavy thread, strong yarn,
or colored string about 8 inches long.
Make the two ends even, but do not make a knot in them.
The 19 X's in the picture show where to put the knots.

Push the needle straight down
through all the layers of the cover.
Then push the needle up through again
about ¼ of an inch away.

Cut off the thread close to the needle and tie the ends of the
thread together in a knot. Make sure it is a tight knot.
Then trim the yarn, leaving the ends about ¾ of an inch long.

Zzzzzzzzzzzzz.

Five

If you have two large pieces of cloth,
you can sew them together to make something to wear.

You can make a bright play skirt or a fancy half-slip,
and you can trim it with lace or fringe or braid or rickrack
or ribbon or anything else that looks nice.

If you do not have enough material at home to make a skirt,
maybe you can buy something you like.

Shopping for material is fun.
There are many colors and patterns and kinds to pick from.
What you decide to buy depends on what you are
going to make.
Cotton in a bright color or a playful pattern makes a fine skirt.
Something soft and delicate is pretty for a half-slip.
Tell the salesperson what you want to make,
and she can help you choose.

How much material you need depends on how big you are
and how wide the material is.

Ask someone to measure you from your waist to below your
knees. (The skirt will not be that long, but you must allow
enough at the top and the bottom for hems.)

You will need to have enough material to cut two pieces,
a front and a back.

You will also need a piece of elastic about half an inch wide
and long enough to fit comfortably around your waist.

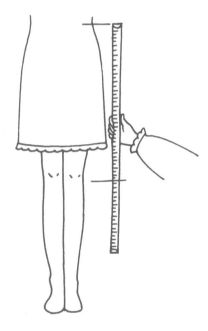

If you are going to buy some trimming, you will need enough
to go all the way around the bottom of the skirt.

Be sure to ask if it can be washed when you wash your skirt.

THIS IS HOW TO MAKE THE PATTERN
- -

This time *you* are the pattern.

Ask someone to measure you again from your waist
to exactly where you want the skirt to come.
(It is hard to do this yourself. If you bend over even a little,
the measurement will be wrong.)

Write down the number of inches.
Add an inch for the casing at the top where the elastic will go.
Add 2 inches at the bottom for the hem.

Then add them up. That will be the length of the
two pieces you will cut.

THIS IS HOW TO CUT IT OUT
- -

Lay the material out flat on a large table
or on the floor if you do not have a table big enough.
Check to see if the material was cut straight across
at the store. You can straighten it by cutting
in the direction of the crosswise threads.

The tightly woven edges on the sides are called *selvages*.

Use a yardstick and measure the correct number of inches
for your skirt along each selvage.
Mark the place with a straight pin.
Then lay the yardstick across the material and put in a row of
pins from one side to the other to make a cutting line.

Cut straight across the material, following the row of pins.
Use the piece you have measured
and cut it out as a pattern for the second piece.
Lay it on top of the rest of the material.
Make the top and the selvages even and put a few pins
around the edges to hold it in place.
Then cut the second piece.
Cut off the selvages because they sometimes shrink in the wash.

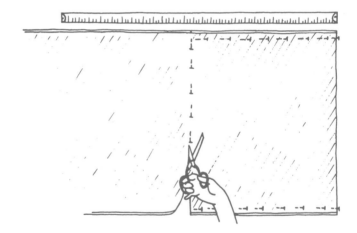

THIS IS HOW TO PUT IT TOGETHER

Put the two pieces of the skirt
or half-slip together
(the way you did the drawstring
bag, with the right sides
on the inside) and pin it
along the two sides.

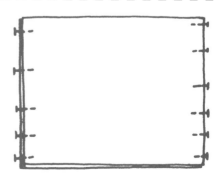

Most seams on clothes are made ⅝ of an inch wide.
If you have your own ruler,
you could mark that place
on it with a crayon
or a small piece of tape.
You will be using it often.

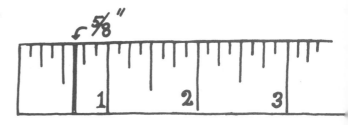

Now measure ⅝ of an inch from the two side edges and mark
the material with chalk or pencil.
Make your marks clear and even,
about every 2 inches,
because this is the seam line
along which you will sew.

Make another mark ¾ of an inch
from the top on one seam.
This will be the opening for the
elastic around your waist.

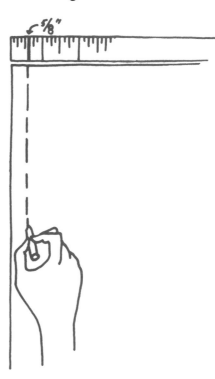

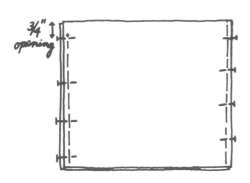

AND THIS IS HOW TO SEW

Thread your needle and knot the ends of the thread.
(Your knot should be as small as a gnat by now!)
Start at the little mark you made at the top
for the opening for the elastic,
and sew all the way to the bottom,
following the line of pencil or chalk marks.

Make your stiches as small and straight as
you can. Try to make them like this – – – – –
so that your skirt will look nicer and last longer.
Then sew the other seam.
Start at the top and sew all the way to the bottom.
Now you can take out the pins.

You are ready to make the casing for
the elastic waistband.
Keep the skirt wrong side out.
Press open the seams on both sides
with a warm iron or with your fingers.
Then fold down an inch at the top and press it.
Next turn under a little bit of the cut edge.
Pin the turned-under edge to the skirt
all around and baste it with large, even
stitches in a different colored thread.

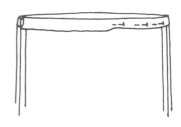

Now you can take out the pins.
Thread your needle, make one end longer than the other,
and put a knot in the long end.
Then sew with little hemming stitches all around the casing.
Pull out the basting stitches.

Now is the time to put the elastic in the waistband.
Pull the elastic around your waist
and hold it so that it feels just right.
It should not be too tight or too loose.
Then add about an inch to overlap.

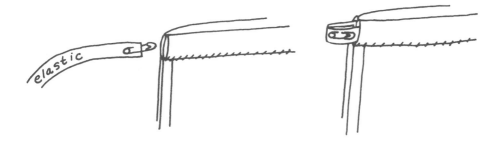

You can fasten a safety pin to one end of the elastic
and use that as a "needle" to pull it through the opening
that you left at the top of one seam. (Be sure to anchor the
other end of the elastic so it doesn't get lost.)
Overlap the two ends about an inch and
fasten them with a strong safety pin.
Then you can take out the elastic
when you wash and iron your skirt.

Turn the skirt right side out and try it on.
It isn't finished yet, but you can see how pretty it will look.
Ask someone to help you decide how long to make it
and to mark the bottom of the skirt all the way around
with pins or chalk and a yardstick.

Take off the skirt and turn the hem
to the inside along the marks.
Fasten it with a pin about every 3 inches and try it on again.
If you use small safety pins to pin up the hem,
your trying-on won't be so prickly.
Look in a mirror.
Is the skirt as long (or as short) as you want it?
Take off the skirt and press the hem carefully.
Then measure 2 inches from the fold of the hem.
Perhaps you will have more than 2 inches left for a hem
or even a little less than 2 inches,
but measure as much as you can for a hem.

A big hem will make the skirt hang nicely, and you can let it
down as you get taller and the skirt gets shorter.
Measure and mark all the way around
the hem with pins, pencil, or chalk.

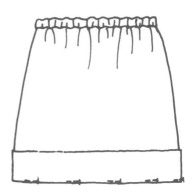

Now cut carefully along the marks.
Turn under a little bit of the cut edge.
Pin the hem to the skirt all around
and baste it with large, even stitches.
Now you can take out the pins.
Thread your needle, make one end of the thread longer
than the other, and put a knot in the long end.
Then make hemming stitches.
Try to make the stitches very small
so they barely show on the right side.
If you don't want to sew the hem,
you can buy hem tape that you iron on.
It goes on quickly and is very nice because when you get taller
and your skirt gets shorter you can peel off the tape with a
warm iron, let down the hem, and iron the tape back on again.

Miss Patch made herself a new skirt.

IF YOU ARE MAKING A FANCY HALF-SLIP

Just follow the directions for making a skirt *except*
if you are going to put lace on the bottom,
cut the slip a little shorter than you want it to be
and make a tiny hem about half an inch deep.

To sew lace around the bottom, lay the top edge of the lace
even with the bottom of the slip, with the right sides together.
(It will look as though you are
putting it on upside down.)
Pin it and baste it.
Then sew the edges together with
very small overcast stitches.
When you have finished,
press the lace down.

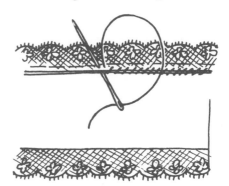

Pretty, isn't it?

Miss Patch thinks so, too.

Now you know how to sew.

You know how to cut out pieces of cloth
and stitch them together to make something.
And you can make some of your own patterns.

Next you will want to learn
to use printed patterns.

On the next few pages are some patterns
for you to try.

You can make them for yourself
or for presents:

    a gingerbread boy doll
    a pincushion heart
    a bath mitt
    a hand puppet

THIS IS HOW TO DRAW THE PATTERNS

Use circles and rectangles to draw the *gingerbread boy.*
Find a drinking glass or a lid to use as a guide,
a large one for the body and a small one for the head.
Overlap the two circles to make a strong neck.
Add rectangles for arms and legs.

Use your imagination to draw a *heart.*
Use your hand to draw the *bath mitt* and the *hand puppet.*
If you are making an *oven mitt* for your mother,
use her hand to draw it.

After you have drawn what you are going to make,
add about half an inch all around for a seam.
Be sure to copy all of the marks from the pictures.
You don't need to cut the pattern out of the paper.
Fold the material in half with the right sides on the inside.
Lay the pattern on top and pin it,
with the pins inside the cutting line.
Then cut it out, following the outside line.
Cut through the pattern and both layers of material
at the same time.

Then take out the pins and take off the pattern.
Put the pins back in to hold the material together.
Copy the marks from the pattern onto the material
with pencil or chalk.

THIS IS HOW TO MAKE A GINGERBREAD BOY

You can use any kind of material, but brown looks
especially gingerbready.

After you have cut out the two pieces,
sew buttons on one piece for eyes, nose, mouth, and jacket.

To sew on a button, first thread your needle,
make the ends even, and knot them.
Push the needle through from the wrong side
and slip the button over it.
Then push the needle down through another hole.
Go up and down about eight times and fasten the thread
by winding your needle in and out of the stitches
on the wrong side.

(If you don't want to use buttons for the face, you can glue on
pieces of felt or bits of yarn after the doll is finished.)

Put the right sides together, pin them, baste,
and sew all around with running stitches.
But don't sew between the two dots on the top of his head.
Wherever it says "clip" on the pattern,
use sharp scissors to make tiny cuts in the seam.

Cut up close to your stitching but not through it.
Turn the doll right side out and stuff it with old stockings
or plastic bags cut into strips.

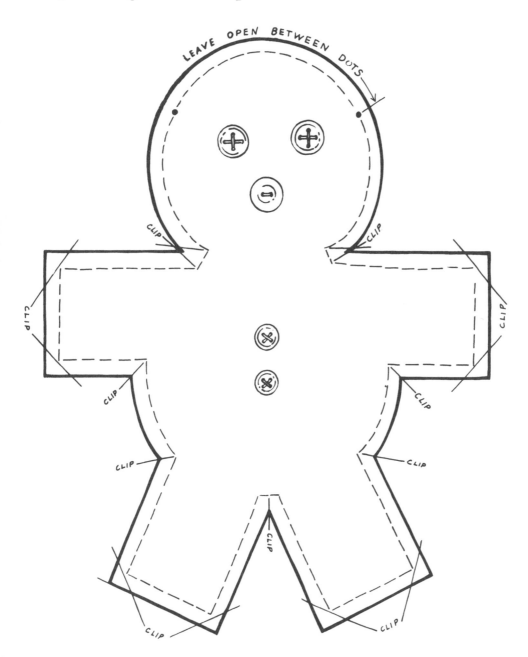

Tuck in the raw edges on the boy's head and sew them shut
with overcast stitches.
This Gingerbread boy makes a lovely toy
for your favorite baby!

THIS IS HOW TO MAKE A PINCUSHION

Red is the very best color of all for a heart, but you could use
any happy color. Just be sure the cloth is strong enough to
take all the jabbing it will get.
After you have cut out the two pieces,
print or write I LOVE YOU on the right side of one piece.
(You could put a name on the other piece.)

Thread a large needle with yarn
or two strands of embroidery thread.
Make one end longer than the other
and put a knot in the long end.
Bring the needle up from the wrong side of the material
at the bottom of the first letter
and sew around each letter, using a backstitch.

Look on page 23 to see how to do it.
Before you cut the yarn at the end of a word,
wind the needle back and forth through a few stitches
on the wrong side so the stitches won't come loose.

Put the right sides of the heart together, pin them, baste them,
and sew all around with running stitches,
except between the two dots.

Make one clip at the top of the heart.
Turn it right side out and stuff it with cotton.
Tuck in the raw edges and sew them shut with overcast stitches.

CLIP

I   LOVE

YOU

LEAVE OPEN

A nice present for someone you like!

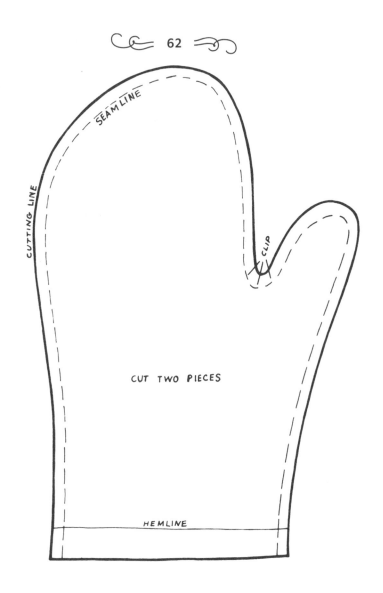

SEAM LINE

CUTTING LINE

CLIP

CUT TWO PIECES

HEMLINE

THIS IS HOW TO MAKE A BATH MITT . . .

Terry cloth is the best material for washing.
You can use a towel or two washcloths for the material.
If the terry cloth you have is very thick,
you might want to cut just one piece at a time.

Pin the pieces together, baste them, and sew all around
(but not across the bottom) with a running stitch.
While the mitt is wrong side out, turn up a little bit of
the bottom edge and then turn it up again to make the hem.
Pin the hem and baste it. Sew it with a hemming stitch.
Clip the curve next to the thumb. Turn the mitt right side out,
stuff it with your hand, and have a good scrub.

OR AN OVEN MITT

You can make an oven mitt for your parents to use in the
kitchen or for barbecuing in the backyard.
Cut the mitt out of heavy material
or make it two or
three layers thick.
Baste the layers together,
then sew the oven mitt
the same way you did
the bath mitt.

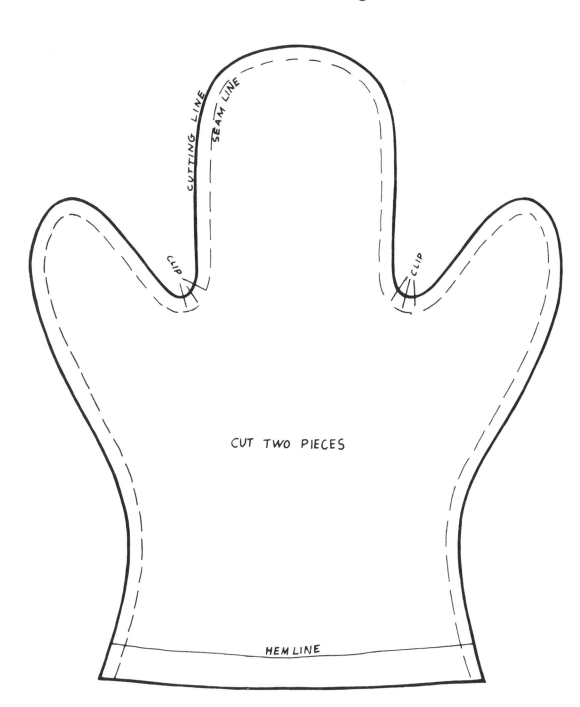

64

CUTTING LINE

SEAM LINE

CLIP

CLIP

CUT TWO PIECES

HEM LINE

THIS IS HOW TO MAKE A HAND PUPPET

Cut two pieces of cloth,
whichever kind is best for the puppet you are making.

Pin the pieces together, baste them,
and sew all around (but not across the bottom)
with a running stitch. Clip the curves.
While it is wrong side out, turn up a little bit of the bottom
edge to the outside, then turn it up again for a hem.
Pin it and baste it.
Sew it with a hemming stitch.

Then draw a face on the puppet with crayon,
or glue on bits of felt or yarn.
Or you can backstitch the eyes, nose, and mouth
before you put the pieces together.

Seven

Miss Patch and Charlie have a friend.
Her name is Elizabeth Anne,
and she is about your age.
Elizabeth Anne likes to play with dolls
and to dress them in pretty clothes.
One day when Charlie was much younger,
she pretended that he was a doll and put
her doll's clothes on him.
Charlie didn't like that one bit.

Soon Elizabeth Anne will
have a birthday.
Miss Patch is sewing some doll
clothes as a present for her.
Here are the patterns Miss Patch is
using to cut them out
and the directions she is following
to put them together.

Charlie hopes very much that none of the dresses fit *him*.

If you have a fashion doll who is 11½ inches tall,
you can make some very stylish clothes for her.

You can make a play skirt, just like the one you made for
yourself, and a sundress, and a long skirt, and a
full-length formal evening gown — all from one pattern.

You can make a school dress with sleeves
from another pattern.
If you cut it short, it will make a beach cover-up
to put over her bathing suit.
Or it will make a blouse to wear with the play skirt
you have made.
If you make it long and sew lace on it,
she can use it for a nightgown.
And if you cut it out of fancy material,
it can even be an evening gown.

Look in your scrap basket
and see what kinds of material you have.
Try to find material that is not too heavy,
so that it will fit your doll nicely.
Try to find material with a small design.
Even tiny flowers will look big on your doll.

You can make a dress look very simple or very fancy,
depending on what material you have and the way you trim it.
If you do not have any lace or velvet material
for your doll's evening dress, use plain cotton.
Then see if you can find some lace or velvet ribbon for a belt
or jewels from a broken necklace to glue on the skirt.
You will also need some elastic, ¼ of an inch wide.

THIS IS HOW TO DRAW THE PATTERNS

These patterns will be easy to copy if you have some graph paper. You can buy it in most stationery stores. If you cannot find any graph paper, it is not hard to make some yourself. Draw lines, half an inch apart, across a piece of plain paper. Then draw more lines, half an inch apart, from top to bottom to make squares. This takes time, especially if you are being careful to make the lines straight and the squares even.

This is how the squares will look.

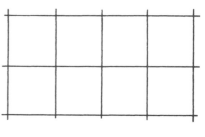

The patterns in this book are drawn on squares that represent ½-inch each. When you copy the patterns, they should be twice as big as they are in this book.

If you are using hand-drawn graph paper with ½-inch squares, copy the lines and marks from each single square in the pattern onto single squares on the graph paper.

Since most store-bought graph paper is printed on ¼-inch squares, you will have to remember to count *two* squares of graph paper for every *one* square in the picture.

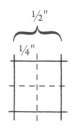

Use a different colored pencil if you have one.
Sometimes the lines you copy
will come between the lines of the graph paper.

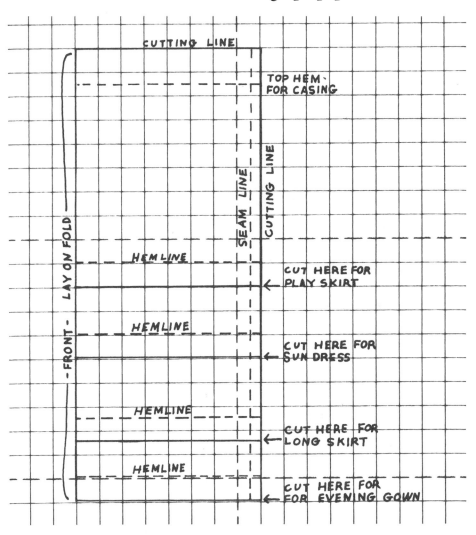

You can use a ruler to help you draw them straight.
Keep counting and drawing until
all the lines and marks have been copied.

If you would rather not use graph paper at all,
you can use gingham material with ¼- or ½-inch checks
and draw the pattern right on the cloth.
Follow the directions for drawing on graph paper.
You can make a play skirt that grows . . .
and grows . . . and grows.

AND THIS IS HOW TO DO IT

Copy the part of the pattern you are going to use.
Cut it out, leaving a little space around it.
Fold the material in half with the right side on the inside.
Lay the pattern on the material
so that the edge marked FRONT is on the fold.
Pin it and cut it out.
Take out the pins and take off the pattern.

Keep the piece folded on the front fold
line with the right side
on the inside.
Pin it and baste it
along the back seam.
Thread your needle and knot one end.
Sew all of the doll clothes
with single thread.

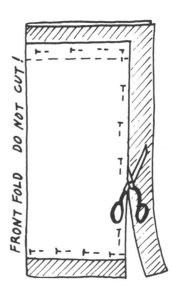

Sew the seam with running stitches as far as the small dot.
Press the seam open with your fingers.

Then fold down the hem at the top to make the casing
and sew it all around with running stitches
that are small on the outside
and bigger on the inside where they don't show.
Turn up the hem at the bottom
and sew it all around the same way.

Cut a piece of elastic 3½ inches long.
Put a tiny safety pin in one end and use that as a needle
to pull the elastic through the hem (the casing) at the top.
Let your doll try on her new outfit.

If you have made a skirt, overlap the ends of the elastic
and pull it tight around her waist.
Sew through the elastic with several stitches.

If you have made a dress, overlap the ends of the elastic
and pull it tight around her chest.
Sew through the elastic with several stitches.

Cut a piece of pretty ribbon about 7 inches long
and tie it around her waist for a belt.

You can make a dress
  or a blouse
  or a beach cover-up
  or a nightgown
  or a robe
with this pattern.

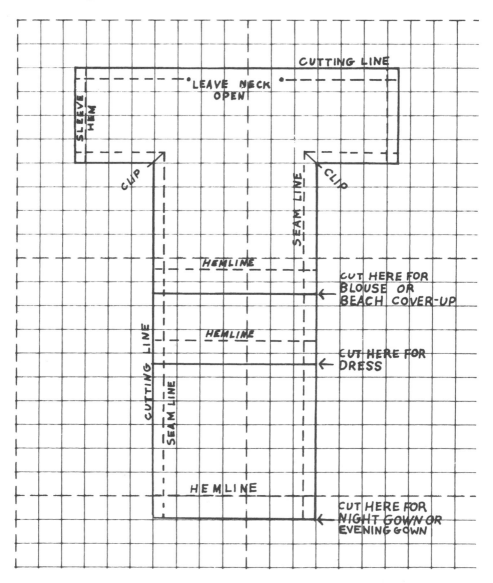

AND THIS IS HOW TO DO IT

- -

Fold the material in half with the right side on the inside.
Lay the pattern on top.
Pin it and cut it out.
Take off the pattern.

Put the two pieces together with the right sides on the inside.
Pin it and baste it along the top shoulder seam.
To make the hem for the neck,
sew the seam with running stitches, but leave it
open between the two dots for the doll's head to go through.
Open the dress along the shoulder seam you have sewed
and press the seam open with your fingers.
The middle part of the shoulder seam makes the hem
for the neck opening. Press that part open, too,
and sew around the neck opening with running stitches
that are very small on the outside and larger on the inside.

Turn up the hem on each sleeve and sew it straight across
with running stitches that are small on the outside.
Put the dress together again with the right sides on the inside.
Pin it and baste it under the sleeves
and along the two side seams.
Sew the seams with running stitches all the way to the bottom.

Turn up the hem on the bottom and sew it all around
with running stitches that are small on the outside.
Sew lace around the bottom of the nightgown.
(Page 55 tells you how to do it.)
Cut a piece of ribbon or heavy yarn about 7 inches long
to make a belt for the dress.

What a well-dressed doll you have!

If you have a baby doll or a little girl doll,
you can make some pretty clothes for her, too.

LONG-SLEEVED DRESS   **SLEEVELESS DRESS**   **PINAFORE WITH LONG SLEEVES**

COAT   **ROBE**   *Charlie*

You can make her a dress with long sleeves and one with
short puffy sleeves and one without any sleeves at all.
You can make her a pinafore to play in
and a coat to go visiting in.
You can make her a nightgown for sleeping
and a robe to wear after her bath.
And you can make them all from one pattern.

If your doll is 12 to 16 inches long,
copy the SMALL pattern on the next page.
If your doll is 14 to 17 inches long and rather chubby,
use the LARGE pattern on page 81.
If your doll is longer than 17 inches,
add an inch around the bottom of the LARGE pattern
and half an inch to the sleeves.

THIS IS HOW TO CUT OUT
ALL THE OUTFITS

Fold the material in half (with the right side on the inside)
so that the pattern will fit on it *twice.*
Lay the pattern on the material, pin it, and cut it out.
Take out the pins and take off the pattern.
You will have two small pieces.

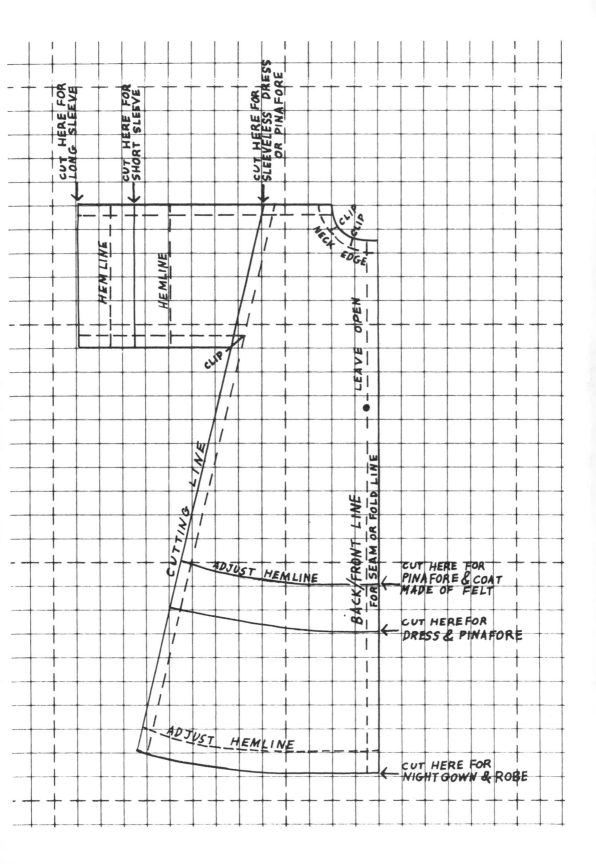

Then cut along the BACK/FRONT line of the pattern,
cutting off the seam allowance,
and lay the pattern on the material again
with the BACK/FRONT line right along the fold.
Pin it and cut it out. Be sure not to cut through the fold!
This time when you take off the pattern you will have
one big piece, making three pieces altogether.

YOU CAN MAKE THE
DRESS WITH SLEEVES

After you have cut it out,
put the two smaller pieces together
with the right sides on the inside.
Pin it and baste it along the back seam.
Thread your needle and knot one end.
Sew all of the doll clothes with single thread.
Then sew with running stitches
from the bottom edge as far as the dot.
Press the seam open with your fingers.
Put the front and back sections together
with the right sides on the inside.
Pin and baste the shoulder seams
and sew with running stitches
from the edge of the sleeve to the curve of the neck.
Press open the seams with your fingers.

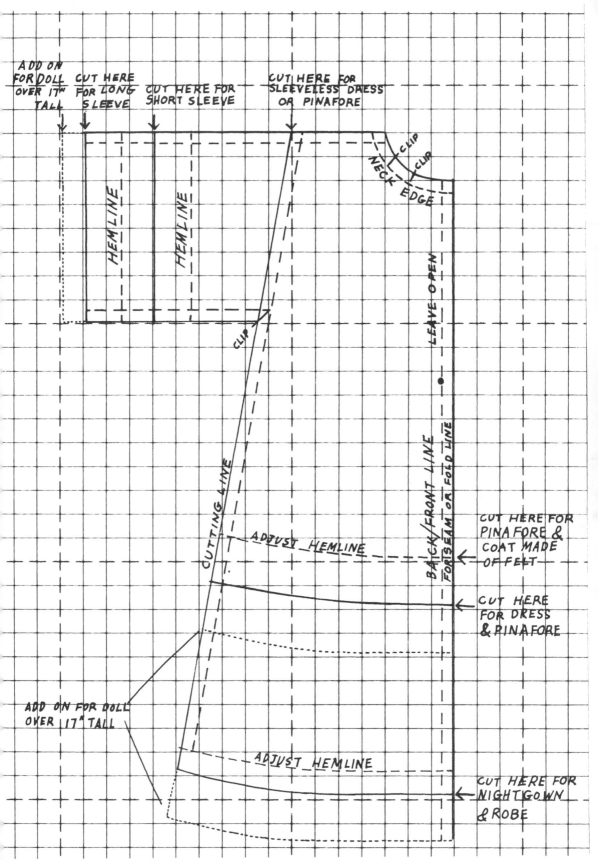

Baste all around the circle of the neck
with small stitches ¼ of an inch in from the edge.
Then with a small pair of scissors
make two little clips between each seam
almost — but not quite — in as far as the basting stitches.
Turn down the hem that curves around the circle of the neck
along the basting stitches.
The cuts make the job easier.
Press the hem with your fingers.
Pin it and baste it.
Then turn to the inside the two parts of the back seam
that were left open above the dot.
Pin and baste them.

Beginning at the dot on the back seam,
sew up along one side of the back opening,
sew all around the circle of the neck,
and sew down along the other side of the back opening
and stop at the dot.
Sew with running stitches that are small on the outside
and larger on the inside.

Pin and baste the side seams
and sew them with running stitches.
Press them open with your fingers.

Pin and baste the seams under the arms
and sew them only as far as the sleeve hemline.
Clip the seams under the arms.
Turn up the hem of the sleeve and press it with your fingers.
Pin it and baste it and sew it all around
with tiny hemming stitches.
If you want to sew some lace around the sleeves,
read on page 55 how to do it.
Then cut two pieces of elastic, ¼ of an inch wide, long enough
to go around your doll's arm with a little bit left over to overlap.
Put a tiny safety pin in one end and use that as a "needle"
to pull the elastic through the hem.
Be sure to fasten down the other end so it doesn't escape.
And have patience!

You may have to try a couple of times
to get the elastic to do what you want.
Then overlap the ends of the elastic
and sew through them with a few stitches.

Try the dress on the doll and decide
where to put the hem. Fold up the hem
and turn under a little bit of the cut edge.

Pin it and baste it and sew the hem with hemming stitches.

Cut two pieces of ribbon about 4 inches long.
Sew one piece to each side of the neck opening
with tiny overcast stitches.

Now try the dress on your doll
and tie a pretty bow at the back of her neck.

YOU CAN MAKE THE DRESS WITHOUT SLEEVES

- -

almost the same way, *except—*

After you have sewed the side seams
and pressed them open with your fingers,
turn under the cut edge of the armhole.
Pin it and baste it and sew it all around
with running stitches that are very small on the right side.

Then finish making the dress.

YOU CAN MAKE A PINAFORE

- -

to wear over the dress with sleeves
almost the same way, *except—*

Leave the back completely open.

After you have pinned and basted
the hem around the circle of the neck,
turn under the cut edges
on each side of the back opening.
Pin and baste them.

Then, starting at the bottom of the dress,
sew up along one side
of the back opening, sew all around the circle of the neck,
and sew down along the other side of the back opening.
Sew with running stitches that are small on the outside.
Finish the hem at the bottom of the dress.

Sew a piece of ribbon to each side of the neck opening.
Measure down 2 inches
and sew on two more pieces of ribbon.

YOU CAN ALSO MAKE THE PINAFORE OUT OF FELT

Felt is harder to cut out because it is heavy.
But it is easy to sew because you don't have to make hems.

When you copy the pattern for the felt pinafore,
do not copy the hem at the bottom
or around the circle of the neck.

Copy the shoulder seam and the BACK/FRONT seam
and the side seams of the pattern,
but don't copy the hem around the armhole.

After you have cut out the pieces, put them together
(there is no "wrong side" to felt)
just as you did the dress or the cotton pinafore, *except—*

There is no hem to sew at the bottom
or around the armholes or the circle of the neck.
You will need to press open the seams with a very warm iron.
Leave the back open.
Sew a snap at the neck and another snap 2 inches below it
to close the pinafore.

THIS IS HOW TO SEW ON A SNAP

First decide where you are going to put the snap.
Half of the snap goes on one part
of the opening on the *outside.*
The other half goes on the other part
of the opening on the *inside.*
With different colored thread,
sew up through one hole and down through the next,
just to hold the halves of the snap where they belong.

Then with double thread,
bring the needle up through the first hole
and make three overcast stitches through the hole and the felt.
Bring the needle up through the second hole
and make three more overcast stitches.
Do this until you have sewed through each hole.
Then sew on the other half of the snap.

If you want to, you can sew a button on the outside,
on top of each snap. Turn to page 58
and read again how to sew on a button.
Go up and down through the button only about three times.
If this were a real "buttoning" button,
you would have to go up and down a few more times,
but you don't want too many threads to cover
the snap underneath.

YOU CAN MAKE A WARM COAT

If you make the coat out of felt,
it will look neat and it will be easy to sew.
When you copy the pattern for the coat,
do not copy the hem at the bottom
or at the end of the long sleeve
or around the circle of the neck.

After you have cut out the pieces, put them together
just as you did the dress with sleeves, *except*—

This time the opening is in the *front,* and there is no hem
to sew on the sleeves or around the circle of the neck.
Sew three snaps on the front of the coat
and sew pretty buttons over them.

If you do not have any felt to make the coat,
you can make it out of corduroy or any other warm material.
But then you must be sure to copy all the hems
on the pattern and add on an extra half an inch to the front,
measuring outside the BACK/FRONT line.
Turn under that extra half an inch on each side
to make a hem for the front opening
and to leave room to sew on the snaps and buttons.

YOU CAN MAKE A CUDDLY NIGHTGOWN

almost the same way you made
the dress, *except*—

You copy the long pattern, and you
do not need to put elastic in the sleeves.
Sew ribbons in the back
to close the nightgown.

AND YOU CAN MAKE A
CUDDLY ROBE TO MATCH

or one out of terry cloth
almost the same way you made the coat, *except*—

You must remember to copy all the hems on the pattern
and add on an extra half an inch to the front,
measuring outside the BACK/FRONT line.

Turn under that extra half an inch on each side
to make a hem for the front opening
and to leave room to sew on three or four snaps and buttons;
or turn under the full ¾ of an inch
and sew ribbons on the front instead.

Elizabeth Anne loves the doll clothes Miss Patch has made, and Miss Patch is so pleased with herself that she has decided to write a book about how she learned to sew.

She's calling it *Miss Patch's Learn-to-Sew Book.*

Charlie approves. Don't you?